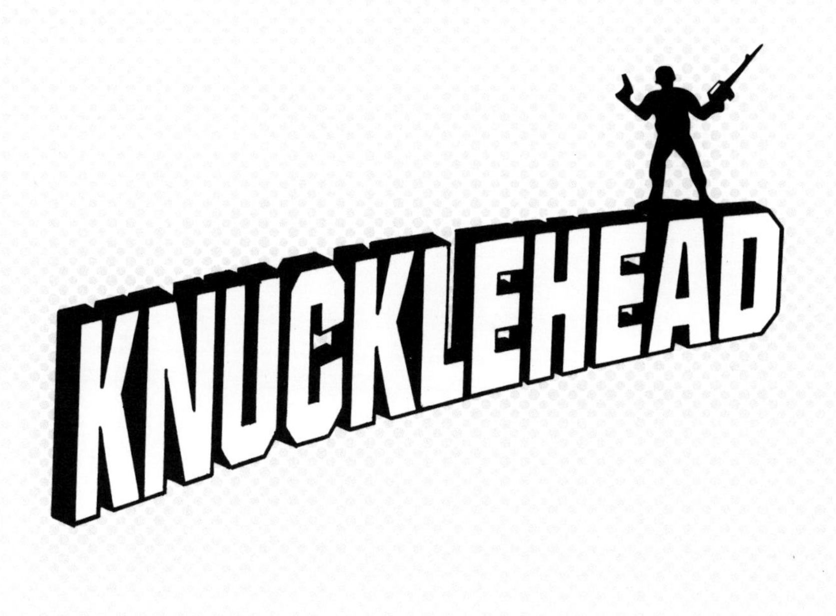
KNUCKLEHEAD

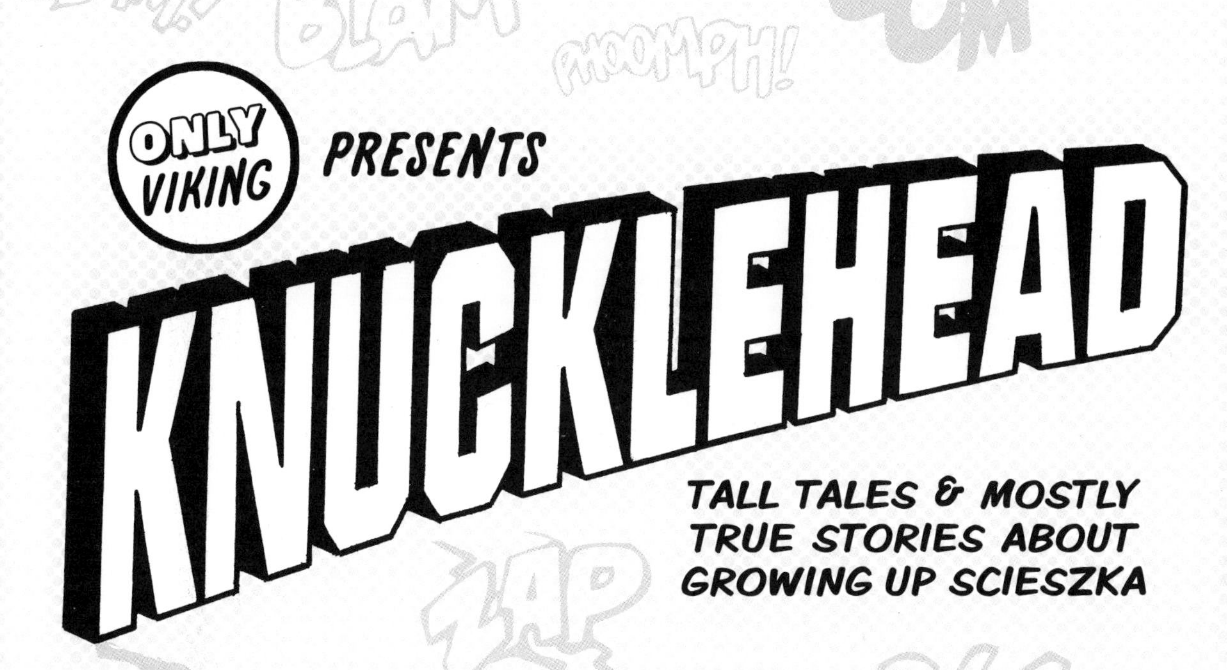

Featuring:

JON SCIESZKA

VIKING
Published by Penguin Group
Penguin Young Readers Group, 345 Hudson Street, New York, New York 10014, U.S.A.
Penguin Group (Canada), 90 Eglinton Avenue East, Suite 700, Toronto, Ontario, Canada M4P 2Y3
(a division of Pearson Penguin Canada Inc.)
Penguin Books Ltd, 80 Strand, London WC2R 0RL, England
Penguin Ireland, 25 St Stephen's Green, Dublin 2, Ireland (a division of Penguin Books Ltd)
Penguin Group (Australia), 250 Camberwell Road, Camberwell, Victoria 3124, Australia
(a division of Pearson Australia Group Pty Ltd)
Penguin Books India Pvt Ltd, 11 Community Centre, Panchsheel Park, New Delhi — 110 017, India
Penguin Group (NZ), 67 Apollo Drive, Rosedale, North Shore 0632, New Zealand
(a division of Pearson New Zealand Ltd)
Penguin Books (South Africa) (Pty) Ltd, 24 Sturdee Avenue, Rosebank, Johannesburg 2196, South Africa

Penguin Books Ltd, Registered Offices: 80 Strand, London WC2R 0RL, England

First published in 2008 by Viking, a division of Penguin Young Readers Group
"Car Trip" first appeared in a slightly different form as "Brothers" in *Guys Write for Guys Read*,
first published by Viking, a division of Penguin Young Readers Group, in 2005

7 9 10 8 6

LIBRARY OF CONGRESS CATALOGING-IN-PUBLICATION DATA
Scieszka, Jon.
Knucklehead : tall tales and mostly true stories about growing up Scieszka / by Jon Scieszka.
p. cm.
ISBN 978-0-670-01106-3 — ISBN 978-0-670-01138-4 (pbk.)
1. Scieszka, Jon—Childhood and youth. 2. Scieszka, Jon—Humor.
3. Authors, American—20th century—Family relationships. 4. Children's literature—Authorship. I. Title.
PS3569.C5748Z46 2008
813'.54—dc22
[B]
2008016870

Manufactured in China • Set in Palatino • Book design by Sam Kim

To Mom and Dad

and

Jim, Tom, Gregg, Brian, and Jeff

-Jon

CONTENTS

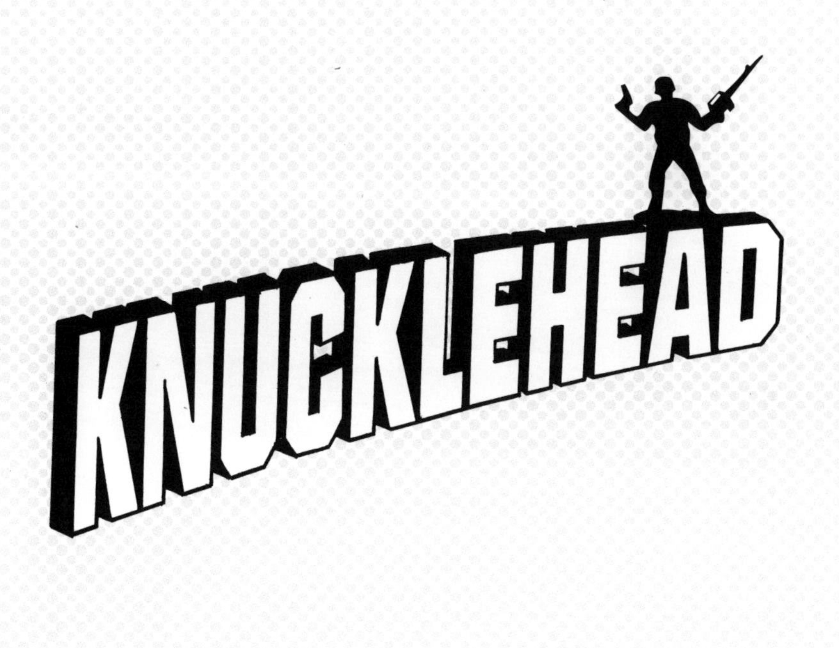
KNUCKLEHEAD

Mom (Shirley) & Dad (Louis)

Jim

Jon

Tom

Gregg

Brian

Jeff

1
BEGINNING

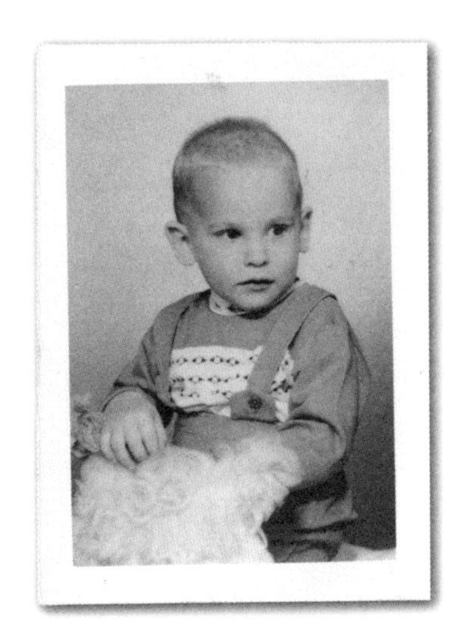

I grew up in Flint, Michigan, with my five brothers— Jim, Tom, Gregg, Brian, and What's-His-Name. The youngest one. Oh yeah—Jeff.

I'm the second oldest. And the nicest. And the smartest. And the best looking. And the most humble.

We didn't have any sisters. All boys. Even our dogs and cats and fish were boys. I'm not sure how that happened. That's just how it was.

My dad, Louis Scieszka, was an elementary-school principal. We didn't go to his school, which was probably good, because being sent to the principal's office would have been weird. But my dad used a lot of his principal skills to run a house with six boys. We had the home version of meetings and rules and schedules.

My mom, Shirley, was a nurse. This also came in handy, because she could tape us up when we ran through windows, fell out of trees, crashed our bikes, stuck a dart in Tom's leg, or broke Gregg's collarbone.

Now that I write for kids, a lot of readers ask me where I get my ideas. I think that's a great question. But I feel like I've never come up with a great answer. The more I think about it, the more I realize that I get a lot of my ideas from all the strange things that happened to me growing up with five brothers.

So here is the beginning of the answer to that mysterious and difficult question: "Where do you get your ideas?"

2

WHO DID IT?

My mom always used to tell us, "Don't wrestle in the living room. You are going to break something."

We would always answer, "Sure Mom."

But one time Jim jumped me . . . in the living room . . . so I put him in a headlock. Jim tried to trip me with a karate-sweep kick. I flipped him over and we both landed *bam!* right on the couch.

The couch, of course, broke. The two front legs snapped right off.

"Oh man," I said. "Mom is going to kill us. What are we going to do?"

We tried propping the couch back up on the broken legs. That worked great . . . until we touched it. Then it fell right down again.

"Don't worry," said Jim. "I know exactly what to say."

My mom walked into the room and freaked out. "What happened to the couch?!"

Jim said, "Uhhh . . . Jon did it."

I couldn't believe he said that.

I said, "I didn't do it. Tom did it."

Tom said, "I didn't do it. Gregg did it."

Gregg said, "I didn't do it. Brian did it."

Brian said, "I didn't do it. Jeff did it."

And Jeff was the youngest. He didn't have anyone else to blame. So he looked around and said, "I didn't do it. Ummm . . . the dog did it?"

That's where I learned it's good to be the one telling the story.

Especially if you didn't do it.

3

HOME, SWEET HOME

Here are me, Brian, Tom, Jim, and Gregg outside our house in Flint, Michigan. It was built right around the time I was born. All the houses on our block were built at the same time. And they all looked pretty much the same.

Our house was a little different, because it had a big fancy metal *S* on the front screen door. *S* for *Scieszka*.

It was great to live in a neighborhood that was still being built, because that meant we had plenty of empty lots and construction sites around us. And empty lots and construction sites meant plenty of ditches for foxholes and trenches, dirt clods for bombs, and scrap wood for building forts.

We had plenty of kids on our block, too. We could always find lots of guys to join in our games of war, cowboys and Indians, and bike demolition derby.

The house itself was pretty small. And every year or two mom would disappear, then come back home with another baby brother wrapped up in a blanket. Because there were six of us, we always had a roommate. And it was always the brother next in birth order. Jim and me. Tom and Gregg. Brian and Jeff. We didn't really have a choice. And no one ever changed.

Jim could be annoying. Like when he would take the bottom bunk bed and kick the mattress above him when I was on top. But I got him back by hanging my hand down like an escaped murderer to freak him out as he woke up.

When Brian and then Jeff arrived, Jim and I moved down to a new bedroom in the basement. We thought it was the coolest place in the whole house. We were by ourselves and closer to the kitchen than anyone else. It was also so cold that we had an electric space heater to use sometimes in the winter.

The twisty metal coils on the heater had a great orange glow when they got hot. Just like the fires we would build with Dad out at the lake.

I guess that's what made me and Jim think we could put out the heater the same way we put out the fires at the lake—by peeing on it.

But when the two yellow streams hit the hot orange coil, things didn't work out so well. Something hissed. Something popped. And the basement was filled with the most awful smell of fried urine.

Jim and I unplugged the heater. We opened the windows even though it was freezing. And whenever our mom asked about the heater, we said we didn't really need it anymore.

4

ROOMMATES

Jim was a pretty good roommate because he was neat and not too much of a pain in the neck like the little brothers. But man, could Jim talk.

I think Jim knew from the time he was four that he was going to be a lawyer. He was always trying to win an argument or make a case why you should agree with him. Jim would talk and talk and then talk some more.

His best pitch ever was the time he tried to sell me my own shirt.

I was looking for a clean shirt to wear. Most of my clothes were in a pile on the floor of my closet. I was digging through the pile, sniffing for one that was not too smelly.

Jim pulled a clean, folded, short-sleeved shirt out of his dresser drawer.

"I really should save this shirt, Jon. But because you need it, I'm going to give you a deal," said Jim.

I found a shirt with only a couple of grass stains on the elbows.

"What's that?" I said.

"This is an excellent shirt, a clean shirt, a lightweight shirt, a short-sleeved shirt," said Jim. "But because you need it, I'm going to give it to you for a bargain price."

I held up a pretty good-looking dark blue shirt. It smelled like the two-week-old socks still hanging on it.

"Look at this shirt. It's a great shirt. Probably the best shirt," said Jim. "And I am going to let you have it, while I wear my same old shirt, for only fifty cents."

I looked at the shirt. It was a great shirt.

"It's perfectly clean," said Jim.

He was right. It was perfectly clean.

I checked my pockets.

"I've only got twenty-five cents," I said.

Jim put the shirt back in his drawer.

"I'm afraid I can't go any lower than forty cents. It's my only clean shirt. I'm going to need it soon. I was going to do you a favor, but I can see it's not going to work out."

I tried on a brown shirt. It smelled even worse than the green shirt.

"Maybe I can get twenty-five cents off Tom," I said. "Let me see the shirt."

Jim handed it over. I tried it on. It fit perfectly. It was clean. It was so . . . familiar.

"Hey," I said. "This is my shirt."

"It was in my drawer," said Jim. "You owe me fifty cents."

"I do not."

"You do too."

"Do not."

"Take it off."

"Make me."

Our legal debate quickly turned into a wrestling match. Jim jumped on me. I got him in a choke hold. We rolled around on our bedroom floor.

So I think it was really me who made Jim a better, stronger lawyer.

5

COOKING

I learned how to cook because I like to stir oatmeal more than I like to pick up dog poop.

Maybe I should explain.

Because there were so many of us, every couple of months my mom or dad would try some new plan to organize us six boys.

Like one spring my mom got tired of us always mixing up our sweatshirts and losing them. She bought six identical blue hooded sweatshirts, and she ironed giant white numbers on the back: 1, 2, 3, 4, 5, 6.

We didn't mix up our sweatshirts after that. But we did manage to lose them.

For a while to make it easier to keep our clothes straight, my mom also tried color coding us. Jim was blue. Blue shirts, blue pants, blue socks. I was brown.

I really grew to hate brown. Even today, forty years later, I still avoid brown clothes.

But the biggest plan was the Family Job Chart.

You might imagine that a pack of boys wouldn't be too keen on washing, cleaning, or cooking. And you would be right. We tried our best to avoid anything we thought was work. Our mission was always to get out of work and get away to play. Which is why my dad came up with the job chart.

The chart listed all the different chores around the house (vacuuming, table setting, cooking, dishwashing, dog feeding, yard pickup) and all our names (Jim, Jon, Tom, Gregg, Brian, Jeff). The idea was that every week each guy would have a different job.

But I hated feeding the dog. The look and sound and smell of that gloppy wet stuff plopping out of the can gave me the willies. The only thing worse than that was the look and feel and smell of what the dog turned the food into . . . and then plopped out in piles all over the backyard.

So to avoid any of the nasty dog work, I would trade jobs with Brian and Jeff whenever they had cooking. Because they were the youngest, they usually didn't get exactly what was going on. I would just tell them, "Brian, you get to feed the dog again this week. Jeff, you get the best outside job this week." I think it helped them become better people.

It also kept me in the kitchen. And the kitchen was the best place to be. Helping my mom cook, I would stir oatmeal, flip bacon, butter toast, peel potatoes, mix cakes . . .

All much better smelling jobs than the dog chores.

And the best added bonus of the cooking job was that you got to eat more. A taste of scrambled eggs here, a bit of toast there. I still love eating raw potatoes with a little salt when I cook.

And the oatmeal. Ahhh. The oatmeal. No place better to be on a cold morning than standing over a huge warm pot of bubbling oatmeal.

From my weeks, months, and years of experience I can now reveal to you the secret of great oatmeal:

Here's what's cookin' JON'S OATMEAL RECIPE Serves 8

Recipe from the kitchen of

1. MAKE A BIG POT OF IT. AT LEAST ENOUGH FOR SIX GUYS PLUS TWO PARENTS.
2. USE THE WHOLE-GRAIN OATS. MIX WITH MILK, NOT WATER.
3. ADD BUTTER AND SALT WHILE IT'S COOKING.
4. STIR IN CIRCLES, STIR IN FIGURE EIGHTS, STIR IN BACKWARDS CIRCLES.
5. REPEAT STEP 4 OVER AND OVER UNTIL THE OATMEAL/MILK MIXTURE THICKENS AND STARTS BLORPING LIKE MINI VOLCANOS.
6. WARM YOURSELF OVER THE STOVE. TAKE A TASTE OR TWO OR THREE. AND BE VERY HAPPY THAT YOU ARE NOT OUTSIDE PICKING UP DOG POOP.

6

MOM

My mom was a registered nurse, which came in very handy for patching up the cuts and bruises that happened every day. She was also the cook, the Cub Scout den mother, the cleaner, the reader, the homework assistant, the schedule manager, the finder of anything lost, and the fashion buyer/maker.

Mom taught me to read, to cook, to make gold spray-painted decorations out of dried pasta and glue, and to hate dressing exactly like anyone else. Because Jim and I were the two oldest, I think my mom had a lot of energy to spend on dressing us up. We have all kinds of pictures of me and Jim in matching shorts and saddle shoes, matching vests, matching coats, matching underwear.

As we added more and more brothers, my mom tried to keep up the matching dressing. We all wore the same red Christmas

vests she made for a few years. But as soon as we were old enough, we tried to find our own clothes, and let the little brothers look like goofy multiple twins.

Where my dad's sense of humor was slow and often unexpected, my mom loved the crazy joke, the fast remark, the wild comeback. When we were home, we always ate dinner all together. And the dinner table was where everyone learned to polish his own sense of humor and timing. My brother Jim would talk as fast as possible, overloading everyone with information and babble (he's a lawyer). I tried to crack everyone up with the strange or racy joke . . . then while they were laughing, make a grab for the last piece of chicken.

But my mom knocked us out with her medical jokes. The first one I can remember that stunned us all was: "Little Johnny stood up in class one day to read his report: 'I saw two dogs running. One ran right into the other one's butt and knocked him off a cliff.' 'Oh Johnny,' said the teacher. 'We don't say butt. We say rectum.' 'Rectum?' said Johnny. 'It darn near killed 'em!'"

Jim and I cracked up. Tom and Gregg looked a little puzzled. Brian and Jeff reached for more potatoes. And that punch line instantly became a family classic. We all used it for years after to answer any question, describe any situation, interrupt any long-winded conversation.

You can still ask any of us, "Wrecked 'em?"

And you can be sure you will get the classic answer: "Darn near killed 'em."

7

DAD

Dad was an elementary-school principal. None of us went to his school. It was on the other side of town. But his being a principal came in handy, because our house was like a school—with kids in six different grades.

We didn't really know it at the time, but Dad was always teaching us. We thought we were just smacking around old lumber, but Dad was teaching us how to use a hammer and saw. We thought we just happened to find books like *The Cat in the Hat* and *Go, Dog. Go!* lying around the house, but Dad was helping us learn to read by surrounding us with books we wanted to read.

Dad was a great golfer. In the summers he ran the Flint Junior Golf program and taught us all how to golf. We never thought of it as teaching, though. We were just playing around with Dad. And we were having fun. We've all played golf ever since. And we have a family golf tournament (named after Dad Lou—the Coupe de Lou Classic) that we've played for twenty-five years.

Where my mom was a wild joke-teller, Dad was more of a quiet joker. One of his best pranks was the April Fool's day when he came down for breakfast wearing his usual suit coat. There was a little piece of white thread on the shoulder. My mom went to pick it off, but it just got longer and longer and longer and longer. He had a whole spool of thread in his shirt pocket. And he had threaded it through his jacket.

But the best thing my dad taught us was how to treat kids with respect. He did this by listening to us. He would listen to our crazy stories, our lame jokes, our wildest ideas. He would listen to every side of any argument.

And I'm sure that's why my brother Brian and I both became teachers. We learned from our dad that kids do have something to say, and that they will say it . . . if you are willing to listen.

8

CROSSING SWORDS

Here's a picture of all six Scieszka brothers dressed up for Christmas. You can tell it's Christmas by the manger scene on the mantelpiece. It was a nice little wooden house with statues of Mary and Joseph, three Wise Men, a mess of animals, and the Baby Jesus (who got put in on Christmas Day).

Mom always tried to make it look nice with banks of cotton "snow." But Jim and I liked to add some extra touches. We would pose the three Wise Men fighting the camels. Or we would sneak Davy Crockett or a couple of army machine gunners into the scene. Maybe a guy with a bazooka hiding behind the sheep. We thought it made a much livelier Christmas story.

This is a pretty classic pose for everyone. Jim, as usual, is doing his best to look the most grown up. He's got a real tie, and he knows it. The rest of us got stuck wearing another one of Mom's experimental fashion ideas.

I couldn't get it together enough to bother arguing, so I'm wearing the experiment. Tom is messing around with something in his pocket and not posing like he's supposed to. Gregg is smiling about a joke he hasn't told anyone but he's sure is very funny. Brian is not happy that he got wrestled into nice clothes and has to sit on half of Gregg's chair. And Jeff, as the youngest, is plopped down in front of everyone else, in his own world, not really sure why he is here, doing weird things with his fingers in his lap.

There aren't many pictures like this of all of us together—mostly because it was such a challenge to ever get everyone together, for anything.

Going to church on Sunday, Mom and Dad would first make

sure Jim and I were dressed and ready. They would put us in the car with Brian and Jeff to make sure they didn't wander off. Then they would go try to corral Tom and Gregg before any of us escaped.

Once we were all in the car, ready to leave, someone always had to go to the bathroom.

"You just went," Dad would say.

"I have to go again," Gregg would say.

And once the idea had been mentioned, it just seemed like a good idea for everyone.

"I'm going, too," Jim would say.

"Me, too," I would say.

"I don't want to pee," Tom would say.

"We don't say 'pee,'" Mom would say.

As a nurse, Mom was big on using the correct terms for bodily functions. We did not "pee." We "urinated." We did not "fart." We "passed gas."

And since it would take forever to wait for six of us to go to the bathroom individually, and because we had the anatomy to make it possible, we would usually go two or three or four of us at a time.

That worked out great for speed. Not so great for accuracy.

During one of our group efforts, Jim and I realized that crossing streams was kind of like sword fighting. And so it was. For every time after.

"Sword fight!" one of us would yell, and we would cross streams back and forth. Tom would join in.

Gregg, Brian, and Jeff were always a lot shorter, and unfortunately for them, had to stand a lot closer to the sword-fighting.

"Mom!" yelled Gregg. "Jim and Jon just peed on me!"

"No," said Mom. "They just urinated on you."

"We didn't pee on him," said Jim.

"No," said Mom. "You didn't urinate on him."

"We were just sword fighting," I said.

"No . . . what?!" said Mom.

"All you knuckleheads just get in the car," said Dad.

9

SCHOOLING

I went to Catholic schools from first grade to ninth grade. I didn't really like the whole idea of going to school. I would have been fine just staying home and playing around. But my older brother Jim got dressed up and went to school. So I knew I would be doing the same thing the next year. That's how the world worked.

Kindergarten turned out to be surprisingly fun. The teacher played the piano and sang. We got to play in sand, color pictures, and take naps.

Once I got to first grade, the school business got serious—

learning colors, numbers, letters, words, science, math . . . grades.

The schools weren't big. But the classes were huge. Look at that picture. There were at least forty kids in every class.

We started every day with a prayer and the Pledge of Allegiance. Then the teacher took attendance. My teachers would usually say "Jon Skizz-zee-kuh? Jon Ski-zeck-kah?" Or just "Jon . . . uh . . ."

I learned to just wait until after Tommy Schmidt's name was called. Then when the teacher said, "Jon—" I would instantly say, "Here."

Scieszka is also a real challenge to spell. So I signed my name "Jon S." until about second grade or so.

The two schools I went to—St. Agnes and St. Luke—were run by nuns. Nuns in full habits. (That's what they called the robes and head covering they wore. And I always wondered why they called them that. Like it was just a bad habit to wear the same thing every day? Or maybe a good habit?)

Most of the teachers were nuns. The principal was a nun. And we learned that nuns were married to God. So there was no arguing with nuns. They were God's wife, so they were always right.

Most of the nuns were pretty scary. We did what they said, because we were afraid they would whack us, or use some secret nun power on us, or tell their Husband to hit us with a bolt of lightning.

But there were friendly nuns. Like Sister Helen Jude. She was the nicest teacher in the whole school. She would laugh at

our knucklehead fourth-grade jokes. She would ask us about the comics we were reading. She wanted to know what we were thinking. And we loved her for that.

Every boy in fourth grade would have married her in a second . . . if she hadn't already been married to You-Know-Who.

So instead, we showed our love by doing whatever Sister Helen Jude did. She liked to draw. We drew. She had beautiful handwriting. We actually worked on our handwriting. She led the boys' choir. So, unlikely as it might seem, almost every guy joined the choir.

Jim, being the oldest brother, always had to be the best and most in everything. He became head choir boy. That's him—second row, sixth from the left. Being second oldest, I was fine with just being in the choir. I'm there in the third row, third from the right. As the third oldest brother, Tom got dragged into a lot of things just because Jim and I were doing them. He's sitting in the front row, fifth from the left.

Under Sister Helen Jude's heavenly direction, we learned to sing—in Latin, in four-part harmony. Hard to believe that she could get those amazing sounds out of our most unlikely group.

The picture is proof that the power of love is stronger than the power of fear.

10

WATCH YOUR BROTHERS

That's what my mom used to tell me and Jim— "Watch your brothers."

So we did.

We watched Jeff roll off the couch.

We watched Brian dig in the plants and eat the dirt.

We watched Gregg lift up the lid on the toilet and splash around in the water.

But we didn't get paid for this babysitting. Until one day Jim and I figured out a great way to make a little money on the job.

We were watching Jeff. He had rolled under a chair and got stuck. We dragged him out and stood him up holding on to the coffee table. And that's when Jeff spotted the ashtray.

We watched Jeff grab a cigarette butt.

We watched Jeff put it in his mouth.

We watched Jeff chew the butt, make a crazy face, then spit it out.

Jim and I cracked up laughing.

Then we gave Jeff another butt and watched him do it all over again.

It was such a great trick that we charged all of our friends ten cents to watch.

It was a great way to watch our brother . . . and make a little cash on the side.

11

STRANGE BOOKS

I learned to read by reading very strange books in school. They were brightly colored stories about a weird alien family. Nothing like my family of wrestling, tree-climbing, bike-smashing brothers. And nothing like the families of any of my friends, either.

This family was always neat. There were a boy, two girls, a mom, and a dad. And they talked in the weirdest way. They repeated themselves a lot. Like they would never say, "Hey, look at that dog." They would say, "Look. Look. See the dog. That is a dog."

The alien kids were named Dick and Jane. Strangest kids I

ever heard of. The little sister was named Sally. The mom and dad called themselves Mother and Father.

When I read the Dick and Jane stories, I thought they were afraid they might forget each other's names. Because they always said each other's names. A lot.

So if Jane didn't see the dog, Dick would say, "Look Jane. Look. There is the dog next to Sally, Jane. The dog is also next to Mother, Jane. The dog is next to Father, Jane. Ha, ha, ha. That is funny, Jane."

Did I mention that Dick and Jane also had a terrible sense of humor?

At home my mom read me real stories. These were stories that sounded like my life. These were stories that made sense. She read me a story about a guy named Sam. Sam-I-am. He was a fan of green eggs and ham.

And then there was the story about the dogs. Blue dogs. Yellow dogs. Dogs that were up. Dogs that were down. Dogs that drove around in cars and met each other at the end of the book for a giant party in a tree. I cheered them on. Go, dogs. Go! I read about them all by myself because I wanted to. Go, dogs. Go!

So I guess I didn't really learn to read by reading about those weirdos Dick and Jane. I learned to read because I wanted to find out more about real things like dogs in cars and cats in hats.

12

NAMING JEFF

By the time we got to brother number six, my mom and dad started running out of steam. It seemed like for quite a while, every year or two, they would come home with another baby. And we'd have another brother.

So after having five of us, I think they just ran out of names. Or maybe they were trying to include us all in the process. Either way, we got to help pick the name for brother number six.

Our plan was to make this worth something. We thought, if we're going to name number six, we should get something out of it. So Jim and I decided we should name him after our next-

door neighbor, Fred Wright. Because Fred had some excellent toy guns. We had a couple. But nothing like Fred. Fred had a machine gun where you could pull the bolt back and then shoot *chukka chukka chukka*. Fred also had a bazooka. A bazooka that could shoot.

Our plan was to tell Fred we had named our brother after him, and hope he would do the right thing . . . and let us play with his best guns.

So that's why our youngest brother is named Jeffrey Fred Scieszka. And that's how Jim and I got to play with some great guns.

13

SORRY, MOM

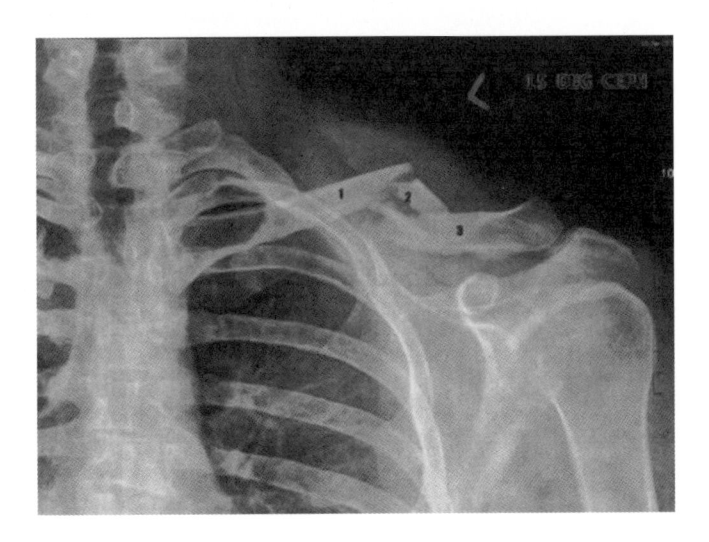

You know that little bone in the front part of your shoulder? The collarbone?

Did you know you can break that bone with just seven pounds of pressure?

We didn't know that, either. But we found out about it when we let our little brother Gregg play football with us.

Well, it wasn't exactly football. It was a game we called "Slaughter Ball." One guy would throw the football up in the air. The rest of us would try to catch it. Then once you caught it, you had to run around and try not to get "slaughtered" by everyone else.

It was a great game because you got to smash into a lot of people and then end up in a giant pile, completely squashing the guy who had the ball.

Gregg was kind of tall and a bit scrawny. He was one of the youngest guys. And his bones must have still been growing. Because one time we were playing Slaughter Ball, and everybody jam-piled on the ball carrier. Gregg got squished somewhere in there. And something more than seven pounds must have squished him, because his collarbone cracked.

We took him home and said, "Sorry, Mom. We broke Gregg."

There's not much doctors can do for a cracked collarbone. They just wrap you up in sling that makes you look like you're wearing shoulder pads. Then you wait for your collarbone to fix itself.

Gregg's collarbone got good at fixing itself. I think we broke him three or four times. We didn't mean to. It just happened playing Slaughter Ball, or Jam Pile, or Swing Jump, or Bicycle Demolition Derby.

Which explains why we have a lot of pictures of Gregg looking like a third-grade pro football player.

14

HALLOWEEN

Dressing up all six of us for Halloween was a real challenge. Mom and Dad couldn't really afford to spend money on six store-bought costumes. And there were too many of us for handmade costumes every year. So we got by with a rotation of four basic costumes. Everyone wore them each at one time or another.

This is me in the classic witch outfit. Pointy black hat, black cape—done. You had to be talked into this outfit before you were old enough to realize that witches were girls.

Costume #2 was what we called the Chinaman. It wasn't very sensitive to real Chinese people. But we had never seen a real Chinese person anywhere in Flint, Michigan. And the costume was easy: Chinese patterned silk pajamas, a few eye pencil marks, and the strangest part—a small Chinese hat with a long black braid of hair attached. Done.

Costume #3 was the Bunny. This is Gregg modeling #3. You can see that in some ways, this was the coolest costume. It was a whole suit. It had the bunny ears attached to the head. It had the bunny feet attached to the legs. It had the bunny tail attached to the bunny butt.

DEC • 63

You can also see from this picture that the problem with Costume #3 was that it was also the dorkiest costume. It made you a bunny. Not at all cool.

The look on Gregg's face shows the realization we each had when we wore #3: "Mom told me this would be a great costume. But now I am dressed up like a bunny. And as soon as I step outside, my friends are going to laugh, and beat on me until I am dead bunny meat."

Costume #4 was the best. The Bum. A ratty old hat, saggy pants, a ripped-up shirt. Black marker on your cheeks for a beard, and you were ready to go. You got to be sloppy and go tell people to give you candy. What a wonderful world. The Bum costume was also sometimes known as the Hobo. And it was always cool.

"But that's only four costumes, and there were six boys," you might say. And you would be right. Our solution was that whoever didn't get one of the real costumes had to be a ghost. Not a real costume. Just two eyeholes cut in a sheet. Hard to see out of, impossible to run in, and guaranteed to get you pushed off many porches and dumped into the bushes. Usually by one of your older brothers. Sorry about that, Brian.

The other solution was whatever was lying around the house. Here is Jeff (or maybe it's Brian?) modeling the prank glasses/mustache/nose. Always funny.

At least we thought so.

The older brothers would also try out some more big-idea costumes on the little brothers. So we would put one of our Boy Scout hats on Brian . . . and take him trick-or-treating as the Smallest Boy Scout in the World. Or we would put the dog collar and leash on Jeff and show him off as the World's Weirdest-Looking Dog.

Once again—always funny.

Or at least we thought so.

15
MOM & DAD

Since my mom was a nurse and my dad was an elementary-school principal, we got to do some pretty weird things that we just thought were normal.

Like when we were in Cub Scouts, my mom was our den mother, so she took us to where she worked. She took us to the hospital. We didn't know where other Cub Scouts went on field trips, so we just went along. I thought we might see X-ray machines, or broken bones, or maybe even doctors operating on patients.

What I hadn't really figured out was that my mom was a prenatal nurse. That's the name for a nurse who takes care of pregnant ladies before they have their babies. So when our field trip got to the hospital, we went into a room with a bunch of pregnant ladies. And pregnant ladies are just not as exciting as broken bones.

My mom and another lady in an official nurse outfit talked to us about the "first nine months of life." I had no idea what she was talking about. I was looking around for an X-ray machine.

After the talk was over, we swarmed around the hospital room, looking for any kind of cool stuff. And that's when my friend Tim found the models. "Look, here's all the guts." Tim picked up the model. He handed it to me. And the whole thing fell apart.

A little baby popped out and bounced on the floor. We suddenly realized we were playing around with models of the insides of pregnant ladies. We freaked out and didn't touch anything else in the room for the rest of the field trip.

Trips with my dad could be just as strange. Every couple of years his school would have an event called Donkey Basketball. They covered the whole gym floor with plastic sheets. They brought in a bunch of donkeys. And the teachers played basketball while riding the donkeys.

Half of the entertainment was watching teachers fall off donkeys. But the best entertainment was watching the donkeys do what donkeys do—drop donkey dumps—in school.

Very educational.

16

BROTHER-SITTING

Babysitters were always kind of a challenge for us. Or maybe we were more of a challenge for them.

Mom and Dad tried putting Jim and me in charge a couple of times. But that didn't work out so well.

Jim and I saw it mostly as a chance to make a little money on the side. So we charged Gregg twenty-five cents for an extra cookie after bedtime. We charged Brian ten cents to have the dog sleep in his room. We generously offered to let Tom stay up an hour later for only fifty cents, but he wouldn't pay. And then he kept getting out of bed. We told him not to. But he kept getting up.

Which is why we tied him up. In his bed. With my dad's ties.

When Mom and Dad found out, they were not too thrilled.

"What if there had been a fire?" said Mom, almost hysterical.

"It would have burned off the ties," said Jim.

"Then Tom could have escaped," I added.

That pretty much ended our babysitting careers for a while. Though it's probably good that we never told Mom or Dad some of our other babysitting techniques. We might have been banned for life.

One of our best tricks was the "Bad Boys' Home" phone call.

If Gregg was being a nut, or Tom was whining, or Brian and Jeff were annoying us, Jim or I would say, "That's it. We're calling the Bad Boys' Home."

BAD BOYS' HOME

123-4567

FLINT, MICHIGAN

We would pick up the phone, dial a random number, wait a second or two, then say, "Hello? Bad Boys' Home? We've got another one for you. Come and pick him up."

We didn't even have to give the address. Because nine times out of ten, a siren would start wailing somewhere in the city. Then everyone would run to bed.

Mom and Dad did try a couple of "outside" babysitters. Like the teenage girl down the block. She was nice. And a lot of fun. She offered to play Cowboys and Indians with us, and even let us tie her up and put her in the closet.

She never babysat for us again.

We were never sure why. But now I realize that two hours tied up in a closet might have been just a little too long.

17

BUYER BEWARE

I loved reading war comics.

Sgt. Fury and His Howling Commandos and *G.I. Combat* were two of my favorites.

G.I Combat told the stories of Lt. Jeb Stuart and his haunted tank. The tank was haunted by the ghost of the Confederate War general J. E. B. Stuart. He always appeared on his horse, looking like a big cloud. And he always gave the tank commander Jeb mysterious warnings that saved him from the Nazis and helped him blow up tons of evil-looking Nazi Panzer tanks.

The lieutenant (and the readers) were the only ones who could see the general. So the tank crew thought their commander was a little crazy, talking to the clouds. But the crew didn't care too much, because they got to blow up a lot of tanks and escape from every impossible jam.

Every story was a little bit of ghost talk and a lot of action. The main tank cannon went *Blam! Whroosh!* and *Blang!*

Bullets bouncing off the metal armor went *Spang! Bwee!* and *Beeang!*

Whram! was the sound of another Nazi Panzer getting its turret blown off.

But just as exciting as the stories were the offers for amazing products on the inside covers. Two-way radios for sixty-nine cents, joy buzzers, trick black soap, prank onion gum, even X-ray specs. And the best of the best were the offers for unbelievable sets of toys.

"Dad, look at this," I said. "One hundred toy soldiers for just $1.25!"

My dad looked over the ad. "That looks great," he said. "But sometimes you have to be careful. They design those ads to make the toys look better than they really are."

"Oh, sure," I said. "And look—you get four tanks and four jeeps and four battleships and eight jet planes and a ton of army men, and it's only a dollar and a quarter."

"How much do you have?" asked Dad.

"Um . . . nothing," I said.

"Well," said Dad, "save your allowance and give it a try."

So I saved my allowance for two weeks. That was a dollar. I popped a quarter out of one of Jim's coin-collecting books. And I had my $1.25. I promised God I would let Jim play with my hundred-piece army a couple of times so He wouldn't have to kill me with an earthquake for stealing.

I filled out the order form. I checked the box marked "Rush the TOY SOLDIER SET TO ME!" And I mailed off my money to:

LUCKY PRODUCTS, INC.
Somewhere in N.Y.
HERE'S MY $1.25!

Then I waited. And waited. And waited.

I kept looking at the ad I had saved on my desk. Eight machine gunners, eight sharpshooters, four bombers. The whole army was even "PACKED IN THIS FOOTLOCKER."

Then one day when I came home from school, there was a brown-paper-wrapped package on the dining-room table. It was addressed to me. Yes!

I scooped it up and ran upstairs to my room.

I ripped open the paper and pulled out a little box. It seemed a bit small. About the size of a deck of cards. I figured maybe they packed each division in a separate box. Army guys in one. Navy guys in another. Jets and tanks and battle cruisers in another.

I opened the little cardboard box, which was marked sort of like a footlocker.

Tiny little bits of dark green plastic spilled out. Each piece was thin as a

dime, and about that tall. For one horrible second I thought the mailman had broken my hundred-piece army. Then I looked more closely at the pieces, and discovered that the truth was even worse—the little pieces *were* my hundred-piece army.

I picked up one skinny bazookaman. He was too skinny even to stand up on his base. Four skinny riflemen, eight very skinny machine gunners. All worthless.

I felt like I'd been robbed. Then I saw a battleship. It was half the size of the bazookaman. The tanks and jets were even smaller!

I couldn't believe it. These were the ugliest, stupidest, just plain wrongest toy soldiers ever. How could someone do that? I didn't even bother to set them up. You can't fight a war with sailors twice the size of their cruisers.

I swept the tiny stupid army off my desk and back into its stupid cardboard box. I was just about to throw it in my trash can when Tom walked by my room.

"What's that?" asked Tom.

"You won't believe it," I said. I pulled the ad off my desk and showed it to Tom. "A hundred-piece army! With four tanks, four battleships, eight machine gunners, eight jet planes, four bazookamen, and more!"

"Wow," said Tom.

"Yeah," I said. "And it's only $1.50 . . . and it comes PACKED IN ITS OWN FOOTLOCKER!"

18

MODEL WAR

Jim and I were model builders. We built scale models of sailing ships, hot rods, WWII destroyers and aircraft carriers, jeeps, half-tracks, tanks, Flying Fortresses, Dam Busters, and Mustang fighters.

When the model airplanes were finished, we would hang them from our bedroom ceiling with fishing line. Then we would swing them around to attack each other. And that looked pretty cool for a while. But eventually it just wasn't cool enough.

Which is why we needed to light them on fire.

Jim took his Flying Fortress. I grabbed my Mustang. And we took them outside to battle.

We crammed the cockpits and the bomb bays full of firecrackers. We twisted all of the fuses together. We counted down to light them at the same time, waited until only the last quarter-inch of fuse was left, then tossed them into the sky.

Blam! Blam! went the explosions.

Splintered pieces of gray and green plastic rained down in a very satisfying mess.

But now we needed more.

One of our neighborhood buddies had once told us that if you tied one of those flimsy plastic dry cleaning bags into knots, then lit it on fire, it would drip hot plastic and make a very cool zipping/bombing noise at the same time.

Jim and I decided it was time to try the Dry Cleaning Bag Attack on our tanks and jeeps. But to be safe, we decided we should stage the attack in the basement.

We set up our tank, jeep, and half-track models on the cement floor in the basement. Jim held up the knotted dry cleaning bag. I lit the bottom knot. It caught fire, started to melt, and then dripped the best melting plastic firebombs *ever*. The zipping bomb noise was just unbelievably perfect.

The German Panzer tank got hit first. Its turret melted into a blob. The U.S. jeep dissolved next under the zipping bombardment. It wasn't until the Sherman tank collapsed that we noticed the cloud of black smoke gathering under the ceiling.

Jim dropped the last of the dry cleaning bag. We scooped up the melted dead. We opened all of the basement windows as wide as they would go.

Months later, Dad asked Tom what those weird black marks were on the basement floor and ceiling.

Tom didn't know. So he said, "I don't know."

And nobody asked us. So we didn't say anything.

Do not try this at home . . .
or anywhere else.

19

PASS IT ON

It's kind of hard to keep six boys in clothes.

You buy one boy a nice suit coat. He looks good in it. Then he grows three inches in two weeks. And now the coat doesn't fit.

What do you do?

Pass it on.

Here you can see the system in action.

I got this jazzy striped coat for my third-grade school picture:

I grew out of it and passed it along to the next brother, Tom, for his third-grade school picture:

Tom grew out of it, and tried to pass it along to brother number four, Gregg. But Gregg couldn't fit in it because he had a cast on his collarbone again (see Chapter 13). So we passed it on to one of our neighbors:

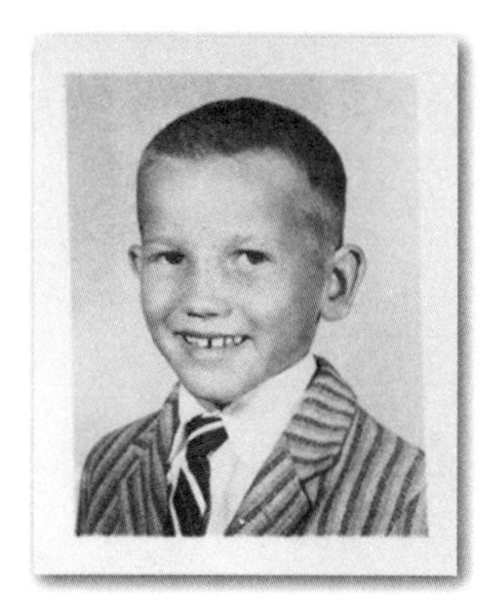

But unfortunately for brothers number five and six, Brian and Jeff, we traded it for a much goofier striped coat.

Sometimes it was tough to be number five or number six.

20
WATCHING

My mom has a picture of Brian, brother number five, when he was about one year old. He's wearing a cute little-guy suit. And his hair is curled in one big wave on top of his head. But the part of the picture you see first is Brian's eyes. They are big. They are brown. And they are watching you.

It's perfect, because that is what the little brothers did. They watched us older guys. They watched us and learned how to do things. They also watched us and learned what not to do.

As a toddler, Brian would watch Jim and me swimming and water-skiing. So of course, almost before he could really walk, Brian was swimming and water-skiing. He became a great swimmer and an amazing water-skier.

Brian watched us older guys hitting golf balls. He became the best golfer of all of us.

Throwing horseshoes, shooting BB guns, riding bikes, throwing Frisbees, kicking soccer balls—Brian would watch us do all of it . . . then do it better himself.

Jim and I didn't really know it at the time, but Brian was also watching us throw apples that splattered on the picture window, jump out of trees, smash up bikes (and later cars), play poker with pals, tell bad jokes, and try out new words we learned on the playground.

Mom wasn't too thrilled when Brian tried out some of the new words he had learned from us at the dinner table. We blamed it on Tom and his bad friends.

But it's interesting that with all of these talents, the one thing Brian didn't have was a nickname.

Jim had hundreds of nicknames. Most of them made up by himself. He was Dr. Justice, J. Bug, J. Love, Chim, Jimmy Love . . . and that was just in one month.

Tom became "Silva Thin" when he got his blond hair buzzed and we could spot his silver head and scrawny body a football field away. "Tomski" also seemed just right for the guy who loved coney dogs and Polish kielbasa.

In our army TV show–watching days, Jim and I named Gregg

"Kirby" after the lanky soldier on one of our favorite shows. That somehow stuck and turned into "Kirby Keefer," then "Kirb," then "Lemonhead."

And Jeff. Jeff and his little pals gave themselves the weirdest nicknames on their own. We didn't have to think up anything to try to bug them. They even spoke their own language. So Jeff was called "Chozz," which Jim turned into "Chuzzlewit," which then became "Chuff," "Chuffrey," and "Chuffrey Fred." "Chozz-bon-dazz" and "Jeff-bon-deff" were two more strange ones from the little-guy language.

But Brian never really had any nicknames that stuck. I didn't, either.

And we both thought that was fine.

21 LESSONS

My mom was an early believer in enriching chil-dren's lives by signing them up for plenty of extra lessons and activities. We thought she was crazy. Why would you want to go to something like school . . . when you weren't in school? I would have been perfectly happy to improve myself with my usual interests—watching cartoons, playing Slaughter Ball in the park, shooting frogs with the BB gun, or just sitting around.

But when Mom announced in her no-questions voice, "You are not just going to sit around all day," I knew I had to pick an improvement . . . or have one picked for me.

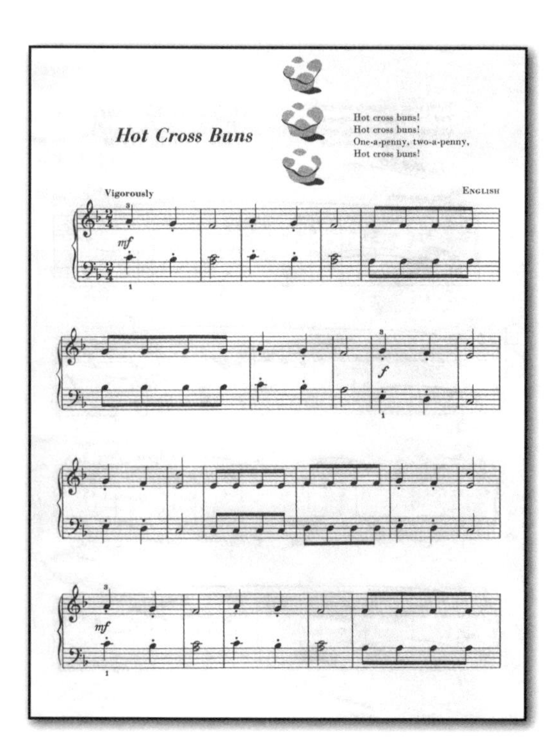

Jim actually wanted to learn how to play the flute. So the whole music-lesson craze was probably his fault. I was assigned the piano, mostly because we already had a piano in the house. My mom played it, and she said I could be the "life of the party" (whatever that was) if I played it, too. Tom chose guitar. Gregg got whatever instrument Dad brought home from the lost-instrument closet at his school. And Brian and Jeff escaped, as usual, with their built-in excuse of being babies.

I liked learning to play the piano . . . for about two weeks. Then it was summer. And I would have rather been anywhere than at the weekly session of me confessing that I didn't get much of a chance to practice, and then having to fake my way through music I hadn't even looked at for a week.

I tried everything to dodge piano lessons. "Oh, is it Wednesday? I forgot." "I don't feel good." "My fingers hurt. They might be broken." Once I even took a nap in the middle of the day—unheard of in our house—and pretended I overslept. The phone had also somehow become unplugged, so no one could call to ask why I wasn't there.

I took French lessons and learned to count to ten in French. I perfected my bowling game under the watchful eye of the wrinkly old guy at the four-lane basement Community Center bowling alley. And I created, in my time at the Flint Institute of Art, perhaps the finest giant clamshell-shaped ashtray ever.

I don't remember much from my hours of piano lessons except where to find middle C. I can only count to ten in French. Haven't sculpted any ashtrays in years. But I still roll a pretty mean bowling ball.

22

THAT WAS WEIRD

A lot of the weird things we did in Catholic school didn't seem that weird at the time. I guess it was because I didn't know anything else. I thought everyone had nuns for teachers. I thought everyone started their school day by going to church. I thought everyone bought pagan babies.

As I grew older, I realized that not everyone went to a Catholic school, not everyone was taught by nuns, and it is almost impossible to explain the whole "pagan baby" business.

But here's what happened. One day our third-grade teacher, Sister Mary Catherine, showed us pictures of starving little African babies. She explained that they were not Catholic like us. They were pagan. But the good news was that if we brought in enough pennies and nickels and dimes, we could buy one of these babies. Somehow they would then be changed into Catholic babies and could eat and not go to hell or something.

We were all a little fuzzy on the details, because the only part of this we heard was the coolest part—whichever group brought in the most money, boys or girls, would get to name the baby.

Us third-grade boys decided that this would be the best

thing ever. We would get to name a baby. We instantly became insane money-raising missionaries. By the end of the month we had begged, borrowed, and stolen enough pennies, nickels, and dimes to buy not one but *two* pagan babies!

Sister Mary Catherine was impressed. Or maybe just stunned.

"My, my. Good work, boys. Let's write down the names of your two babies. The names of the apostles—Matthew, Mark, Luke, and John—are very nice."

"We've already decided on our names," said Billy Wright, our boy spokesman. "We're going to name our pagan babies Al Kaline and Bill Freehan."

"But," said Sister Mary Catherine, "those aren't apostles."

"Heck no," said Billy. "They're the best Detroit Tigers ever. Freehan will definitely hit .300 this year. And Kaline is gonna get thirty homers for sure."

All the boys nodded. This was true.

"Well," said Sister Mary Catherine, "Matthew and Mark will be fine names." And then, in thick black marker, under the pictures of two pagan babies she wrote MATTHEW and MARK.

It was like Billy hadn't ever said anything. Like all of us boys weren't even there.

"But—" said Billy.

"You may sit down," said Sister Mary Catherine.

"But . . . but . . ." said Billy.

"In your seat, Mister Wright," said Sister Mary Catherine.

And that was that. As usual with the nuns, there was no discussion. We were stunned.

After that, most of the boys never bothered to collect any money for pagan babies. What was the point? So every month, the girls won. And every month, the teacher's-pet girls got to name the pagan baby.

Somewhere in Africa today, there are a bunch of guys named Matthew and Mark and Luke and John. And there are even more girls named Mary Anne, Mary Elizabeth, and Mary Catherine.

There should be two guys with the coolest names ever.

But we got robbed.

Matthew

Mark

Luke

John

23

GRAND-PARENTS

Our grandparents were from a different world. They were born before there was even 1900 in the date. That's before there were such things as computers, TVs, or even cars. So when we went to visit the grandparents, we always felt like we were on a different planet.

These are my mom's parents, James and Emmy Marchand. James died before we were born, so we never knew him. But my brother Jim and I spent a lot of time with Nana (Emmy) because we would go and stay with her every time my mom went to the hospital to have a new baby brother.

Nana lived in Detroit. And her house was different. She had soap that smelled like flowers. She had fancy glass things on her tables. She had an alley behind her house. And that was the coolest thing, because that's where Jim and I could shoot our arrows . . . the arrows we had talked Nana into buying for us.

"Are you sure your mom and dad will let you have bows and arrows?" Nana asked in the toy store.

"Oh yeah," said Jim.

"Of course," I said.

That wasn't exactly true. But it was true that we had been wanting bows and arrows. And nobody got any eyes poked out. So it all worked out okay.

And these are Grandma and Grandpa Scieszka. We didn't know their names when we were kids. We just knew them as Grandma and Grandpa. They were both born in Poland, then came to the United States and met each other here.

They both taught themselves to speak English. Grandma's English was pretty good. Grandpa's was not so good. He kind of freaked us out, because he would sit in his chair, smoke his pipe, and say things we couldn't understand.

Grandma cooked delicious chicken. She grew flowers and vegetables in her garden. She kept hard candies in glass bowls in her living room. And we thought that was the best idea ever . . . until we tasted the candy. It tasted awful. Like medicine. But every time we visited, Jim and I would try another one. They always tasted terrible. So we would spit them out and put them back in the bowl. That's probably why the candy pieces all stuck together in one big lump.

Grandpa had his own chickens and the occasional turkey that

he raised. He kept bleached-out skulls of big fish he had caught nailed to the wooden posts in his garage. He made his own wine.

We never did understand Grandpa, but my dad did teach us some Polish. We learned how to say "please" and "thank you" and count to five. And we loved counting to five because in Polish you count:

Jeden . . .

Dwa . . .

Trzy . . .

Cztery . . .

Pięć . . . which you pronounce *pinch!*

And then pinch your little brother as hard as you can.

24

PLAY

We played a lot of games on our own in our neigh- borhood. Some were regular games like baseball and basketball and football. But a lot of games we made up—like Ghost Rider and Slaughter Ball and Black Tiles.

To play baseball we would just take a ball, a bat, and our gloves to the park across the street from our house. We would make home plate in one corner of a grassy field. And the sound of the ball cracking on the bat would bring out our friends.

If there weren't enough players for two teams, we would make the right side of the field closed. Everything right of second base was out-of-bounds. So each team needed only a pitcher, a shortstop, and a left fielder.

Or we would play 500. One guy batting. Everyone else fielding. One hundred points for catching a ball on the fly. Fifty for a one-hopper. Twenty-five for a grounder. First fielder to reach 500 got to be the next batter.

But our best games were the ones we invented ourselves. To play Ghost Rider, you rode your bike under the monkey-bar arch, grabbed the bars overhead, and swung up off your bike so it kept rolling with nothing but . . . a Ghost Rider.

Ghost Battle was two Ghost Riders crashing into each other.

Ghost War was launching as many Ghost Riders as we could fit under the arch at the same time.

The scariest game was Black Tiles. It wasn't really a game. It was more like an adventure. A challenge. A dare.

Black Tiles was played at a spot about half a mile from our house, where the Flint City storm sewers emptied into the Flint River.

A giant pipe, just big enough for a twelve-year-old boy to walk into, stuck out of the side of a steep sand riverbank. Kids told stories that this pipe was connected to the sewer system that ran under all of Flint. You could go anywhere in the city, without anyone knowing you were there.

The only way to get to the opening was to walk across another pipe that bridged a ten-foot-deep (that looked like a hundred-foot-deep) ravine. This pipe was covered in black tiles.

I'm pretty sure our parents told us that we weren't supposed to go in there. But we all remembered our moms saying don't go in there *alone*. So we went together.

The walk across the pipe was scary enough to make even the local tough guy, Pete Deaners, quiet.

When we stepped into the shady, cool black opening we hooted and laughed—partly to hear our voices echo, but mostly to scare away the rats and one-eyed murderers and slimy monsters hiding in the shadows of our imagination.

The smell wasn't bad. But it wasn't good. Kind of like an old bathroom mixed with a barn . . . and a garbage dump.

The safest way to walk was to straddle the trickle of water and who knows what else running down the middle of the pipe. The daring way was to run on the sloped side of the pipe, hopping back and forth across the stream of muck.

We were brave explorers, secret agent spies. We were headed deep under the city.

We walked and hopped in the ever-darker pipe. Our voices and the faint splashing of water echoed all around. Deaners, of course, ran daring style, side to side. We were headed to the inside of the earth. But Deaners slipped. His foot slid on the slime. He fell with a splash.

Deaners screamed. We all screamed. We ran like mad, spilling out of the pipe.

The sun never looked so bright.

The air never smelled so fresh.

We ran back across the black-tiled pipe. We hopped on our bikes and pedaled as if mad hobos with machetes were chasing us, laughing and yelling the whole way.

And then we did it all again the next week.

25

LAW OF THE PACK

I always liked the part of the Cub Scout oath where we promised to "obey the Law of the Pack."

It seemed like a promise to do what we usually did—run around like a bunch of wild animals.

Signing up for Cub Scouts was a lot like signing up for church. It wasn't really my idea. And it wasn't really a choice. It was something Mom and Dad thought was a good idea. Jim was already doing it. So I did it, too.

And once you sign up for Cub Scouts or church, you sign up for the whole deal. No asking any questions. Just learn all the rules and do what you are supposed to do.

I became a Wolf Scout when I was eight. Jim had already been a Wolf for a year. So he had already taught me a lot about the Cub Scouts in his usual big-brotherly way.

"Look at this, Jon. I've got this cool uniform and you don't."

"Why do you have to roll up a dishtowel and tie it around your neck?" I asked.

"That's a neckerchief, stupidhead. And it's the Law of the Pack."

"Oh yeah," I said.

To earn a Wolf badge you also promised to "be square" and "follow Akela." I was never exactly sure who this Akela guy

was, or why he wanted us to be square. But I did know that Wolf Scouts were supposed to follow the Law of the Pack by doing things like swimming, tying knots, building Popsicle-stick letter holders, making Indian stuff, and learning how to properly sharpen your knife.

Yes, your knife. Because every eight-year-old boy needs a sharp knife, right?

I did learn how to properly sharpen my knife. And Jim and I only accidentally cut Tom once, when we were playing a knife game called Mumbly Peg where you drop your knife and stick it in the ground, and we told Tom not to get too close but he did anyway.

I also learned how to track animals, build snares, make papier-mâché heads, chop wood, weave four strands of plastic into a whistle-holding lanyard, paddle a canoe, signal Morse Code, shoot arrows, identify birds, name constellations, safety-proof a home, cook over an open fire, and obey the Law of the Pack in a million different ways that still come in handy.

26

NUMBER 6

There are a lot of advantages to being one of the oldest in a big family. You get more food. You get newer clothes. You get more attention. You get to beat up on the smaller brothers.

It's kind of a sliding scale of benefits, moving down from oldest to youngest. You can see it in our scrapbooks.

Jim and I (#1 and #2) have giant scrapbooks packed with everything—birth announcements, every report card from kindergarten on, every birthday card we ever got, lopsided drawings from first grade, all of our birthday candles, sappy poems from fourth grade, the gum I was chewing when I won a Junior Bowling Tournament, individual pictures of each of us walking to school, riding our bikes, eating birthday cake, brushing our teeth, or just standing there looking adorable.

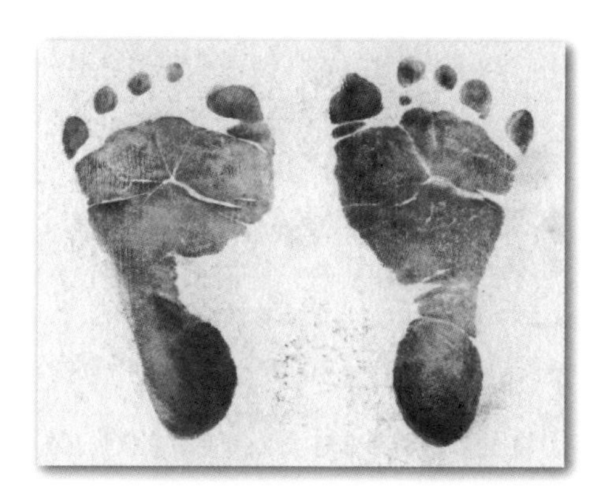

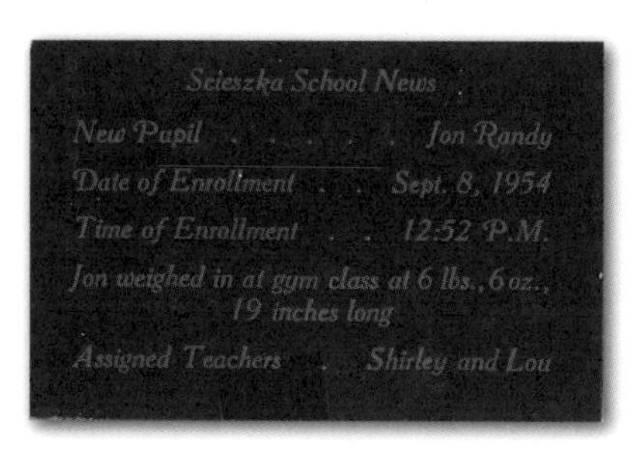

Scieszka School News

New Pupil . . . . . Jon Randy

Date of Enrollment . . Sept. 8, 1954

Time of Enrollment . . 12:52 P.M.

Jon weighed in at gym class at 6 lbs., 6 oz., 19 inches long

Assigned Teachers . . Shirley and Lou

DIOCESE OF LANSING
REPORT CARD
ELEMENTARY SCHOOLS

Catholic education seeks to prepare your child for what he is to be and for what he is to do in this world so as to attain the sublime end for which he was created.

St. Agnes
School

Pupil Jon. Scjeszka

Grade 3 School Year 19 62 19 63

Teacher Sister Eunice SSJ

Tom (#3) and Gregg (#4) have birth announcements, a few birthday cards, some of their report cards, and a handful of pictures.

We're pretty sure that the baby photo in Brian's (#5) scrapbook is him. And he does have his school photos.

Jeff (#6) is found mostly as the smallest guy in group pictures.

But the younger brothers did have some advantages.

Jim and I had to sign up for everything. We were Cub Scouts, Boy Scouts, altar boys, and choir boys.

Jim (#1) was driven to be first in everything. He was an Eagle Scout, Head Choir Boy, Chief Altar Boy, and class president.

I (#2) made it to Life Scout, just below Eagle Scout. I was in the choir for a couple of years. And I knew our class president.

Tom (#3) was in Cub Scouts for a few years, wearing Jim's pants that were a bit short for him. He joined the choir for one year. Was an altar boy for another year. And had heard there was a class president.

Gregg, Brian, and Jeff might have been in Cub Scouts, listened to the choir, and watched the altar boys at church.

The younger guys also got to stay up late, weren't dressed alike, didn't have to always wear rubber boots in the rain, and could watch whatever TV show they wanted and eat sugar cereal in the living room if they felt like it.

So I like to think they had it a lot easier than I did.

27

RANDOM READING

I learned a lot from reading random books around our house. My favorite books for random reading were the Golden Book Encyclopedias. They had lots of illustrations, short sections of reading, and tons of maps and diagrams. You could open any one of the books and find something short and good.

Every state in the U.S. had its own entry and its own map. The maps showed the regular stuff like towns and rivers. But even better—tiny little pictures pinpointed that state's industries and resources. So Michigan had a little car next to Detroit. Montana had little sheep stamped all over the map.

I was amazed that so much information could be packed into a picture. It was like reading without reading.

Same with the diagrams. You could see the whole mollusk family, learn the parts of a bivalve, compare the heights of the world's mountains. All from looking at pictures.

There just seemed to be so much information to know. I soaked up as much of it as I could.

I also learned a lot from watching TV and reading *MAD* magazine. I learned mostly that the stories from TV or *MAD* were somehow different from encyclopedia and book stories.

"Yes, Sister Elizabeth. The main character in this book reminds me a lot of Curly from the Three Stooges. He is always getting beat up by Moe, but he is the funniest and— What book are the Three Stooges from? Oh, they're not in a book. They're on a great TV show where Moe and Larry and— What? Oh. TV shows are sinful? Um, well . . . the other character is kind of like the Coyote in Road Runner because— No, Sister. Coyote and Road Runner. It's a cartoon. Oh. Cartoons are sinful, too? Well, the other character in our book is also kind of like the spies in Spy vs. Spy. They are always tricking each other by— Yes, Sister? No, Sister. It's not a TV show. No, Sister. It's not a cartoon. They are little stories without any words. Yes, Sister. In a magazine. *MAD* magazine. I see, Sister. Probably sinful, too. So. Umm. Well. Ahhh. The characters in this book . . . aren't like anything else I know."

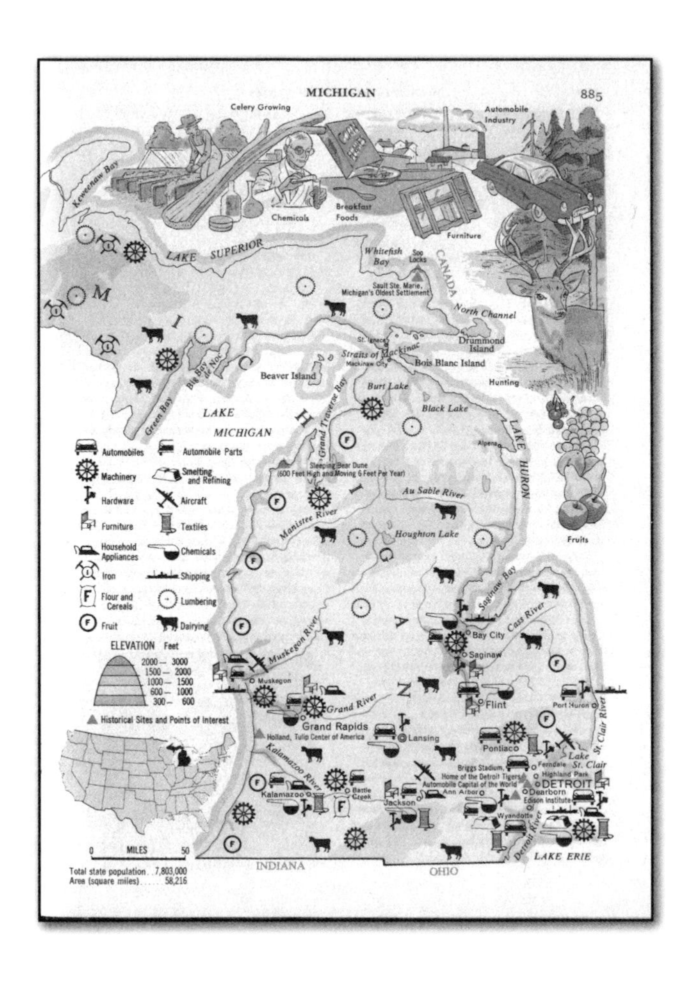

So I learned to not mention TV or *MAD* magazine or cartoons in school ever again. But I still think they were some of the best and funniest and craziest stories around.

Moe would bop Curly on his bald head, pull Larry's wild curly hair, and stick a crowbar up anybody's nose to pull them along. And the classic Three Stooges move was the two-finger poke in the eyes, which always made a great *boink!* sound.

"That show is too violent," said Mom. "I don't think you should be watching that."

"We wouldn't do anything that dumb," we told our mom.

But we did learn how to spin around on the floor like Curly.

And of course we had to poke Tom and Gregg a few times, just to see if we could make that great *boink!* sound.

28

BIRTHDAY

My birthday is in September—which doesn't work out really great for presents. If you can help it, don't have your birthday in September.

And it's not just in September, but early September. Like right when you have to go back to school September. The worst part of September.

I mean, it's bad enough that summer is over and you have to go back to wearing school clothes, getting up early in the morning, doing homework, eating that nasty food for lunch . . . I don't have to tell you how bad that whole going-back-to-school thing is.

But the worst part was, since my birthday was in early September, I would get . . . well, things that didn't seem like birthday-present things. They were things like pencils, notebooks, new socks. Back-to-school kind of presents.

I always wished my birthday was in June. Then I could get something useful. Like a Frisbee or a BB gun, a new fishing rod, a harpoon I could use to stab fish in the lake and then eat them.

It never worked out like that though. My birthday was in early September. So I got socks. Lots of socks.

29

WAR

We told our little brother Tom not to follow us because we were going to war.

Tom followed us anyway.

"Mom said I could," said Tom.

"Mom's not going to be the one who takes a dirt clod in the side of the head and runs home crying," said Jim.

It was the middle of summer. Builders were putting up new houses on the empty block at the end of our street. The dirt lots were covered with foxholes and trenches and wood—perfect for war.

"You're gonna get hurt," I said.

"No I won't," said Tom.

"Yes you will," said Jim.

"No I won't," said Tom.

Jim and I ran down the street as fast as we could.

Tom ran after us.

We dove into our dusty foxholes and started piling up ammo—fist-sized chunks of dried dirt. Perfect dirt-clod grenades.

Jim pulled the pin on one with his teeth (just like we'd seen on our favorite TV show, *Combat*). He chucked the grenade half-sidearm, half-overhand, just like Sarge did.

It flew through the air and landed *Bam!* on a sheet of plywood with a perfect noise and puff of smoke.

I heaved another round and made an excellent *Thoop!* mortar sound.

Bam! Puff of smoke.

"Hey, Scieszka!" someone yelled from behind a pile of dirt.

It was Fred and Bobby D. from our block.

"Snipers," said Jim. "We'll have to take them out."

I nodded. "Roger."

Jim and I launched an all-out attack of dirt grenades, dirt bombs, and dirt machine-gun fire. All with perfect sound effects.

Fred and Bobby D. returned fire. *Bam! Boom! Bam!*

We ducked down in our trench.

"We have to outflank them," said Sergeant Jim.

"What are you doing in that hole?" said Tom.

I looked up at Tom standing at the edge of our foxhole just in time to see an incoming dirt-clod round pop him right in the side of the head. *Bam!* It made a great puff of smoke.

Tom half crouched, half sat down. Jim and I looked at him. He looked like he was going to cry.

Two more dirt clod bombs dropped behind us.

Tom didn't cry. He jumped into the foxhole.

"Charge!" yelled Jim.

And we did.

30
I SWEAR

One day in fourth-grade science class, Bill M., our resident wise guy, gave some kind of wise-guy answer to a question from Sister Chopper. (Chopper wasn't her real nun name, but that's what we all knew her as.) I don't remember any details about the answer, but Chopper's reaction was something we remembered and passed on for years. Chopper, who was very short but very wide, took wise-guy Bill by the front of his shirt and slid him up the blackboard until his feet were off the ground. She then calmly instructed him on how to answer in her class and slid him back down to the floor.

Only crazy people goofed around in Chopper's class.

The nuns and their habits spooked me as a kid. But I was a good reader and a good student, so I didn't get in too much trouble with them . . . until fifth grade, when all the boys got in trouble. One of the girls told the principal, Sister Mary, that the boys were swearing on the playground. So everyone had to stay after school. And we couldn't leave until we had written all of the swear words we knew down on a piece of paper with our name on it, and handed it in. To our teacher—a nun.

Now this was a problem. Because we had been taught in religion class that nuns were married to God. So how were we supposed to write down swear words and give them to God's wife? That sounded like a sure way to burn in hell.

Most of the girls in class wrote down their name, and then handed in their papers with *hell* and maybe *damn* listed. They got to go home.

The first boy walked up with *hell* and *damn* written on his paper. "Go back to your seat," said Sister Margaret Anne. "You know more."

How did she know? We were dead. There was no way we could write down all the bad words we knew. But we weren't getting out of there without writing something else. Soon the room was all boys, each of us trying to figure out how to write swear words to a nun.

I wrote *hell*. I wrote *damn*. Then I was stuck. It didn't look like much of a list. I added *stupid, doofus, butt,* and *goober*. This was looking better. I added *head* to the *stupid* and wrote *stupidhead.*

Divine inspiration. I could add *head* to everything and double my list.

I wrote *doofushead, butthead, gooberhead, damnhead,* and *hellhead*. Then I realized I could combine all of the words to make new words that weren't any worse than the originals. I wrote *stupid-hell, gooberbutt, doofusdamn,* and *hellbutt.*

Now, *there* was a list.

I walked up to Sister Margaret Anne's desk. I handed in my list. The universe stopped while she read it over and looked up at me.

"That will be enough," said Sister Margaret Anne.

And it was.

I walked out of school, waiting to be run over by a bus driven by an angry God. But I guess he liked my invented swear words, or didn't mind me swearing at his wife, or both, because I made it safely home.

31

JON'S SIDE OF THE MOUNTAIN

Summer was the best. Because summer was when all the Scieszka brothers got to run wild . . . in the wild.

My grandfather (my mom's dad) had built a little cottage on a hill overlooking a couple of acres of land on a lake in Michigan, not too far from where we lived in Flint. So in the summer, we would basically move out there.

At the beginning of each summer, my mom would set a kitchen chair outside, then buzz the hair off all of us. We'd take off as buzzheads in June, and not get rounded up, a bit more shaggy, until September.

The lake was a perfect place to become wild men.

We all learned to swim there. Jim and I built tree houses along the shore. We hunted minnows, crayfish, and frogs in the water. We used them as bait to fish for sunfish, bass, and tiger muskies built like torpedoes with teeth.

We would track raccoons and deer, hunt turtles, dive to the bottom of the lake, cook crayfish tails and birds' eggs over our open fires, tattoo our skin with dark walnut stain and red berries, fight apple wars, whittle spears, make bows and arrows, and live as crafty woodsmen . . . at least until the dinner bell rang.

Then we would all charge back up the hill and into the cottage for gigantic meals and even more gigantic stories of all our adventures.

Since there wasn't any TV out at the cottage (and not much service even when there was a TV), rainy days would drive us to do crazy things. Like read the random collection of oddball paperbacks and summer books that had built up in corners over the years.

I read *Field & Stream* magazines, Reader's Digest Condensed Books, joke books, detective novels, *Popular Mechanics*, dusty classics, comic books, and World War Two service manuals. But in this mad heap of writings, I found two treasures: *My Side of the Mountain* and *The Swiss Family Robinson*.

Both of them were written for me. They were my manuals of what I knew I was meant to do—survive in the wild. And survive in fine style.

I spent hours in the woods, looking for that

perfect tree to live in, scanning the skies for the hawk I would raise and train to hunt my food.

I searched out perfect spots for the houses I would build from my shipwreck. I salvaged fishing tackle and made plans to stockpile gunpowder and plenty of rope.

Summer was the time when we got to be the original wild explorers of the land. We named the constellations. We read the signs of the clouds. We heard the message of the redwing blackbird at dusk, the call of the crickets and frogs in deep night.

And then all too soon, the days would grow short, the weather turned cool, and September arrived with school and schedules, clunky shoes and uncomfortable clothes to tame the wild men of the great outdoors.

32

STOP BREATHING MY AIR

In the Scieszka family history, some lines became instant classics. They were so good, or so bad, or so weird that we saved then . . . and repeated them over and over and over again.

"Wrecked 'em? Darn near killed 'em" (see Chapter 6) was one of those classics. Youngest brother Jeff came up with the other most famous.

We were all packed into the family station wagon. Mom and Dad in front. Jim, Jon, Brian, and Jeff in the next seat. Tom and Gregg in the way-back seat. It was hot. Traffic was slow. Barely a whiff of any breeze. The whole pile of us six squirmy boys were smashing, poking, and punching each other.

"Move over," said Tom, elbowing Gregg.

"Get out of my space," said Gregg, kneeing Tom.

"You're squashing me," said Brian, under Jim's elbow.

"Hey," squeaked Jeff, pushed down on the floor mat. "Stop breathing my air."

"What?" said Jim.

"Stop breathing my air," came the smallest voice from somewhere under our feet.

Jim and I cracked up. "Stop breathing my air," we chanted. "Stop breathing my air. Stop breathing my air." And so "Stop breathing my air" became a family classic.

If someone bugged you, you would warn them: Stop breathing my air.

If someone acted stupid, you could correct them: Stop breathing my air.

If you were asked a question, you could always answer: Stop breathing my air.

It still works today, a good forty years later. Why?

Stop breathing my air.

33

CAR TRIP

Of all the Scieszka brother memories, I believe it was a family car trip that gave us our finest moment of brotherhood. We were driving cross-country from Michigan to Florida, all of us, including the family cat (a guy cat, naturally), in the family station wagon. Somewhere mid-trip we stopped at one of those Stuckey's rest-stop restaurants to eat and load up on Stuckey's candy.

We ate lunch, ran around like maniacs in the warm sun, then packed back into the station wagon—Mom and Dad up front, Jim, Jon, Tom, Gregg, Brian, Jeff, and the cat in back. Somebody dropped his Stuckey's Pecan Log Roll on the floor. The cat found it and must have scarfed every bit of it, because two minutes later we heard that awful *ack ack ack* sound of a cat getting ready to barf.

The cat puked up the pecan nut log. Jeff, the youngest and smallest (and closest to the floor) was the first to go. He got one

look and whiff of the pecan-nut cat yack and blew his own sticky lunch all over the cat. The puke-covered cat jumped on Brian. Brian barfed on Gregg. Gregg upchucked on Tom. Tom burped a bit of Stuckey lunch back on Gregg. Jim and I rolled down the windows and hung out as far as we could, yelling in group-puke horror.

Dad didn't know what had hit the back of the car. No time to ask questions. He just pulled off to the side of the road. All of the brothers—Jim, Jon, Tom, Gregg, Brian, and Jeff—spilled out of the puke wagon and fell in the grass, gagging and yelling and laughing until we couldn't laugh anymore.

What does it all mean? What essential guy wisdom did I learn from this?

Stick with your brothers. Stick up for your brothers. And if you ever drop a pecan nut log in a car with your five brothers and the cat . . . you will probably stick *to* your brothers.

34

FIRE

There is something about boys and fire that is like fish and water, birds and air, cats and hairballs. They just go together. They always find each other.

I would try to find any reason to light those big wooden stick matches—helping Dad with the barbeque, helping Mom with the old stove at the lake, making sure the matches still worked by lighting them in the driveway. We were hypnotized by fire.

But our chance to be real pyromaniacs was the Fourth of July, when the adults actually asked us to light matches, sparklers, firecrackers, and bottle rockets.

One year when Jim and I were teenagers, our Wild Uncle Al (whose name was just Al, but everyone always seemed to put the "Wild" in front of the "Uncle") was with us out at the lake.

Wild Uncle Al was Mom's younger brother. He had been a paratrooper in the Eighty-second Airborne Division. Which means he had jumped out of airplanes and knew how to do all kinds of other amazing things.

Wild Uncle Al had driven a surplus jeep he built with his brother into the lake . . . to see if it really would float like everyone said it would. It didn't.

Wild Uncle Al had wrestled a pony to the ground . . . because someone said he couldn't. He could.

Wild Uncle Al had a parachute tattoo and showed us how to do a paratrooper salute.

So when Wild Uncle Al said, "You guys want to make a mortar?" Jim and I gave the only answer possible.

Wild Uncle Al grabbed a short metal pipe. He rammed one end into the sand. He lit a firecracker and dropped it into the pipe. He dropped a rock in on top of it.

"Hit the dirt!" yelled Wild Uncle Al.

Boom! went the firecracker.

Phoop! went the rock shooting out of the pipe.

The rock flew in a huge smoking arc out into the lake.

"*Wow!*" went Jim and I.

"Wow."

See Knucklehead Warning on page 56.
You are not Wild Uncle Al.

35

HAPPY BIRTHDAY TO YOU . . . OR US

I always thought I got lame presents because my birthday was right at the start of the school year. But now that I think of it, my dad and mom got even lamer presents.

My dad's birthday is on Christmas Eve. So we always thought it was funny to give him a salt shaker on his birthday . . . and the pepper shaker on Christmas.

One sock for his birthday . . . the other sock for Christmas.

One birthday cuff link, one Christmas cufflink.

Wiffle ball, Wiffle bat.

Golf tees, golf balls.

Ha, ha, ha.

But we really reached new lows in gift-giving for my mom.

We were all boys. We had no idea what a girl might want. For a few years we used to spend our $1.50 down at the drugstore to buy the shiniest-looking necklace or bracelet. Mom always seemed to like the treasures when she unwrapped them. But I don't remember ever seeing her wearing them. Then we decided perfume was a good Mom gift. Lots of years of very powerful $1.50 perfume followed.

Then one summer day, Jim and I were in the store looking for a good Mom birthday present. Jim picked up a Moonlighter Glow-in-the-Dark Frisbee.

"This is amazing," said Jim.

"We could really use one of those," I said.

"Let's get it for Mom," we both said.

We did. And we started a new tradition of getting Mom exactly what we wanted for that summer.

Mom's best birthday presents were baseballs, a pro-quality volleyball net, a new set of horseshoes, beautiful fishing lures, and the coolest slalom ski ever.

And I think she was glad—glad we had stopped buying her cheap perfume and plastic jewelry.

36

WHAT'S SO FUNNY, MR. SCIESZKA?

The voice flew across the room and nailed me to the back of my seat.

"What's so funny, Mr. Scieszka?"

The voice belonged to Sister Margaret Mary. And it had just flown across our fifth-grade religion class at St. Luke's Elementary School to find me in what I had thought was the safety of the back row.

"What's so funny?" I repeated, trying desperately to stop laughing.

I knew the correct answer to this question was, "Nothing, Sister."

"I'm sorry, Sister," was also a very good reply.

And nine times out of ten, ninety-nine times out of a hundred, I would have used one of those answers. But that day in fifth-grade religion class, something happened. That day I reached a life-choice fork in the road.

My friend and back-row pal, Tim K. had just told me the funniest joke I had ever heard. The fact that he had told it while Sister

Margaret Mary was droning on about our future place in heaven or hell only made it funnier.

Now I was called out.

I saw two life paths laid out clearly before me. Down the one path of the quick apology lay a good grade for religion class, a spot in heaven, maybe even sainthood if things worked out later in life. Down the other path lay the chance of a very big laugh . . . though mixed with punishment, maybe a note to my parents, quite possibly one mad God and forever in hell.

A good grade in religion class is always a good thing in Catholic school. I knew that. But I also knew this was a really funny joke. I was torn between going for the A and heaven, and going for the laugh with a chance of hell. Both were right in front of me.

So when Sister Margaret Mary asked her next question, "Would you like to share it with the rest of the class?" I chose my life's path.

"Well, there's this guy who wants to be a bell ringer," I begin. "But he doesn't have any arms."

Sister Margaret Mary's eyes pop open wider than I have ever seen them. The whole class turns to look at me and the train wreck about to happen. Even my pal Tim K. is shaking his head. Nobody in the history of St. Luke's Elementary School has ever chosen to "share it with the rest of the class." But I feel it. I have to do it. It is my path.

"The priest who is looking for a good bell ringer says, 'You can't ring the bells. You don't have any arms.'"

The faces of my fellow fifth-graders are looking a bit wavy and blurry. "'I don't need arms,' says the bell-ringing guy. 'Watch this.' And he runs up the bell tower and starts bouncing his face off the bells and making beautiful music."

Half of the class laughs. I'm not sure if it's out of nervousness or pity. But it's a lot of laughs.

Sister Margaret Mary's eyes open impossibly wider.

Light floods the classroom. I can't really see anybody now. I can only feel the punch line building. I head toward the light.

"So the bell-ringing guy goes to finish his song with one last smack of his face, but this time he misses the bell and falls right out of the tower. He lands on the ground and is knocked out. A whole crowd gathers around him."

The whole fifth-grade religion class has gathered around me. It is a feeling of unbelievable power mixed with terror for a low-profile fifth-grader like myself.

"'Who is this guy?' the villagers ask."

I feel the whole world pause for just a single beat, like it always does before a good punch line.

"'I don't know his name,' says the priest. 'But his face rings a bell.'"

I don't remember the grade I got in fifth-grade religion class. But I do remember the laugh I got. It was huge. It was the whole class (except Sister Margaret Mary). It was out-of-control hysterical. It was glorious. And it set me on my lifelong path of answering that classic question, "What's so funny, Mr. Scieszka?"

GROWTH IN SKILLS AND SUBJECT MATTER

PERIODS

Subject	1	2	3	4	Final
Religion		C	C	C	C
Reading		a	a	a	[illegible]
Spelling		a	a	a	a
Arithmetic		B	B	a	B
English		B	B	B	B
Handwriting		a	a	B	a
History-Geography					
Science		B	B	B	B
Art		B	a	B	B
Music		B	B	B	B
Health and Safety		B	B	B	B
Honor Points					
Days Absent		1½			
Times Tardy					

A—Superior 95 - 100 B—High 88 - 94 C—Average 80 - 87 D—Poor 70 - 79 U—Unsatisfactory Below 70

GROWTH IN HABITS AND ATTITUDES

A — Always B — Usually C — Sometimes D — Seldom

Teacher's Evaluation 1	2	3	4		Parents' Evaluation 1	2	3	4
				SOCIAL HABITS				
	B		B	Respects Authority		A		
	B		a	Works and Plays Well with Others		B		
				WORK HABITS				
	B		a	Follows Orders Promptly and Accurately		B		
	B		a	Does Required Assignments		A		
				PERSONAL QUALITIES				
	B		B	Accepts Responsibility		B		
	B		C	Manners — Courtesy — Politeness		B		
	B		a	Personal Appearance		B		

Parent cooperation is essential to educational growth. Parents are asked to check growth in attitudes and habits (as they observe it) in column right. These outcomes of education are the measure of character.

37

LEAVING HOME

Jim went away to Culver Military Academy in Indiana for high school. Everyone always asked if he had been bad. But Culver wasn't that kind of military academy. It was a great school with amazing teachers . . . that also happened to have swords and guns and cannons and uniforms and a real black horse cavalry. So of course Jim thought it would be a great place to go to school.

I never gave it much thought. Jim was the oldest, and always a hard-charging guy who would try just about anything. And we had always loved playing war and setting up our Civil War soldiers and building model tanks and ships and jets. So why not?

If I had any thought—it was that I really liked having a room of my own.

When Jim came back from Culver for the summer, he had changed. He was even cockier than he used to be. He had more muscles. He looked adults in the eye and shook their hands firmly. He took a shower every day. Sometimes more than one.

He tried to tell me and Tom that now he was so strong, and knew so many new wrestling moves, he could take us both on. At the same time.

This was just too much. We went down to the basement and started a monster brawl. Scrawny Tom jumped on Jim's back. I went for his legs. We crashed into stacked boxes of stored Christmas ornaments.

Jim trapped Tom in a deadly scissors hold with his legs. I went for a headlock. We rolled over the pile of dirty laundry heaped by the washing machine.

Jim was pretty strong. And he had learned some new moves. But nobody was giving up. We finally wrestled to a standstill.

"Okay," said Jim.

"Okay," I said.

"Oww," said Tom.

That's when I started thinking, *Maybe I should go to Culver, too.*

In tenth grade I did go to Culver. In true knucklehead style, I hadn't really thought much about what it would be like, or if it would be right for me. It just kind of happened. I applied. I got enough scholarship money. And I went.

So in September, when my mom and dad and all the brothers drove Jim and me down to Culver and unloaded us, each with our giant footlocker of regulation T-shirts, underwear, socks, and sheets . . . I sat there suddenly realizing, *I'm not home anymore. Whatever I do is up to me.*

I probably should have asked Jim a few more questions about Culver. I sort of knew that everyone wore the same uniform. But all of the time? Marching in formation to breakfast, lunch, and dinner? In the rain. In the dark. In the snow.

Culver turned out to be the most amazing place. It was the place where I learned to think for myself. It was the place where I learned to really truly read, to write, to learn how to learn.

And, though I don't use the skills much anymore, I also learned how to make a bed you can bounce a quarter off, and fold my underwear exactly four inches across.

38

KNUCKLE-HEADS

The first time I heard the name Knucklehead, it wasn't being used as a particularly good name. I think it was my dad, finding that his toast tasted like melted green plastic army man, who first asked the question, "What Knucklehead put an army man in the toaster?"

The answer was Jim. He was trying to get one of his riflemen to aim a little higher. But that didn't seem like the best answer. So Jim, me, Tom, Gregg, Brian, and Jeff all said, "I don't know."

Over the years, there were a lot more questions.

"What Knucklehead left his bike out in the rain?"

We didn't know.

"Who was the Knucklehead throwing the tennis ball against the aluminum siding?"

We didn't know.

"Which of you Knuckleheads drank the last of the milk and put the empty carton back in the refrigerator?"

We didn't know.

"What kind of Knucklehead would put a window fan on the floor, then stick his toe in it?"

Okay, that was Tom. And there was no denying it, because he was the one with the bandage on his toe.

Eventually the name Knucklehead became just the most common name, and the best one for referring to the whole group. As in:

"Come on, you Knuckleheads, get in the car."

"Stand still and look at the camera, Knuckleheads. Fingers out of noses."

"Get out of the water now, you Knuckleheads!" was just so much easier, and much quicker than saying, "Jim, Jon, Tom, Gregg, Brian, Jeff, get out of the lake now because it is raining and lightning bolts are crashing in the trees all around you."

And the name has mellowed into something even kind of soft and cuddly. Or at least as soft and cuddly as six brothers can get. Now it's something like:

"It's been great seeing all of you Knuckleheads."

"It sure is quiet without all of you Knuckleheads running around."

"And which of you Knuckleheads took a bite out of the middle of the turkey last night, and then filled the hole with stuffing?"

We still don't know.

3, 1, 2, 4, 6, 5

NOT YOUR USUAL INDEX

AFter Culver, young Knucklehead Jon went on to college, where he met the woman who became his wife. They moved to Brooklyn, New York, and raised their two kids there. In New York, Jon wrote stories, painted apartments, and taught elementary school. He published his first story for children, ***The True Story of the 3 Little Pigs!,*** in 1989, and has been writing for kids ever since.

The rest of the Knucklehead brothers grew up to become lawyer, manager, sales executive, teacher/principal, and eye doctor scattered around the country. Jon is still the nicest, smartest, best looking, etc. . . . and was recently named by the Library of Congress the first National Ambassador for Young People's Literature.

So now he has diplomatic immunity.

At least that's what he says.